FARM EXPLORER

Can You Climb a Beanstalk?

QUESTIONS AND ANSWERS ABOUT FARM CROPS

by Katherine Rawson

CAPSTONE PRESS
a capstone imprint

Published by Pebble Sprout, an imprint of Capstone.
1710 Roe Crest Drive, North Mankato, Minnesota 56003
capstonepub.com

Library of Congress Cataloging-in-Publication Data
Names: Rawson, Katherine, author.
Title: Can you climb a beanstalk? : questions and answers about farm crops / by Katherine Rawson.
Description: North Mankato, Minnesota : Pebble, [2022] | Series: Farm explorer | Audience: Ages 5-8 | Audience: Grades K-1 | Summary: "Fruits, vegetables, grains, and dairy—farms have them all! What crops do farmers plant? How do they grow? Kids can find the answers to all their questions about how farmers grow the foods we eat in this interactive Pebble Sprout series"— Provided by publisher.
Identifiers: LCCN 2021970048 (print) | LCCN 2021970049 (ebook) |
ISBN 9781666349207 (hardcover) | ISBN 9781666349245 (paperback) |
ISBN 9781666349283 (pdf) | ISBN 9781666349368 (kindle edition)
Subjects: LCSH: Crops—Juvenile literature. | Farms—Juvenile literature.
Classification: LCC SB102 .R39 2022 (print) | LCC SB102 (ebook) | DDC 633—dc23/eng/20220111
LC record available at https://lccn.loc.gov/2021970048
LC ebook record available at https://lccn.loc.gov/2021970049

Editorial Credits:
Editor: Kristen Mohn; Designer: Sarah Bennett; Media Researcher: Julie De Adder;
Production Specialist: Katy LaVigne

Image Credits:
Getty Images: Anna Solovei, 28, ChViroj, 10 (top), imagenavi, 6, Karin de Mamiel, 12, Nednapa, 10 (bottom), Richard Clark, 13, SCGstudio, 23, Stockbyte, 11 (climbing boy), zlikovec, 15 (back); Shutterstock: AlexLMX, 19, Alf Ribeiro, 3 (bottom left), alfredogarciatv, 3 (middle right), 32 (bottom left), alula.JCpro, 31 (top right), andregric, 3 (middle left), Anek Sangkamanee, 3 (top left), Anna Chavdar, 31 (bottom right), Chanintorn.v, 26, Creativa Images, 30 (left), Danny Smythe, 17 (raisins), Darios, 32 (bottom right), David A Litman, cover (bottom middle), Deyan Georgiev, 18 (bottom), Digital Media Pro, 4, Eric Isselee, 30 (right), Ewa Studio, cover (bottom right), Flutes, 9 (peapod), goccedicolore.it, 14, Ioan Panaite, 29 (tractor), Janis Blums, cover (beanstalk), Jeka, cover (boy), Jenson, 24, Konstantin Mironov, 27 (eyes), Krailurk Warasup, 9 (peanuts in peapod), Lukasz Szwaj, 18 (top), MiulyPhotography, 21 (palm tree), Naruden Boonareesirichai, 5 (corn), Nat YS, 22, Natallia Ustsinava, 3 (middle), Noel V. Baebler, 8, nulinukas, 27 (potatoes), Odua Images, 16, oksanatukane, 3 (top middle), Oleh11, 9 (bottom), Olga Pasynkova (background), back cover and throughout, Oliver Denker, 11 (beanstalk), Peter Hermes Furian, 31 (top left), pjhpix, 25, powell'sPoint, 3 (bottom right), Protasov AN (bee), 29, 32, Romariolen, 20, schankz, 5 (ears), sevenke, 17 (back), 29 (back), Thon Varirit, 32 (top left), Trutta, 31 (bottom left), Unikyluckk, 7, Vector Tradition, 15 (front), Vitalfoto, 21 (strawberries), Yana Tatevosian, 3 (top right), YummyBuum, 5 (faces), Zeljko Radojko, cover (bottom left)

Farmers raise all kinds of delicious fruits, vegetables, and other crops for us to eat. Crops grow in different ways—on bushes, trees, vines . . . and even under the ground!

Let's find out about different kinds of crops on a farm. Read each question and try to guess the answer. Then turn the page to learn the answer.

Did you guess right?

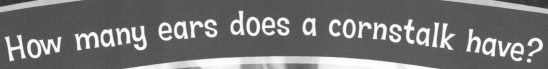

How many ears does a cornstalk have?

Usually a cornstalk grows only one or two cobs—also called ears—of corn. But that's still a lot of kernels. One ear can have up to 1,200 kernels of corn on it.

Are carrots always orange?

We are used to seeing
orange carrots, but carrots
can be other colors too. Some
are purple, red, yellow, or even white.
But a carrot of any color tastes about the same.

Crunch!

Do peanuts come from peas?

Peanuts and peas come from different plants, but they are both members of the legume family. Peas grow on vines.

Peanuts grow underground, next to the plant's roots.

Can you climb a beanstalk?

Only in fairy tales! Pole beans actually grow on vines. Farmers put poles in the ground for the vines to climb up. Some can grow quite high—10 feet (3 meters) or more!

How tall can a sunflower grow?

5 ½

5 ft

4 ½

4 ft

3 ½

3 ft

Sunflowers come in all sizes. The tallest ones can be more than 16 feet (4.9 m) high. That's taller than many houses!

Does lettuce have a head?

Yes, it does! Some kinds of lettuce form a large, round ball of compact leaves. The ball is called a head. Each plant grows one head.

Raisins are just dried grapes.

The harvested grapes are laid out in the sun to dry. After two to four weeks in the sun, they become dry, wrinkly raisins.

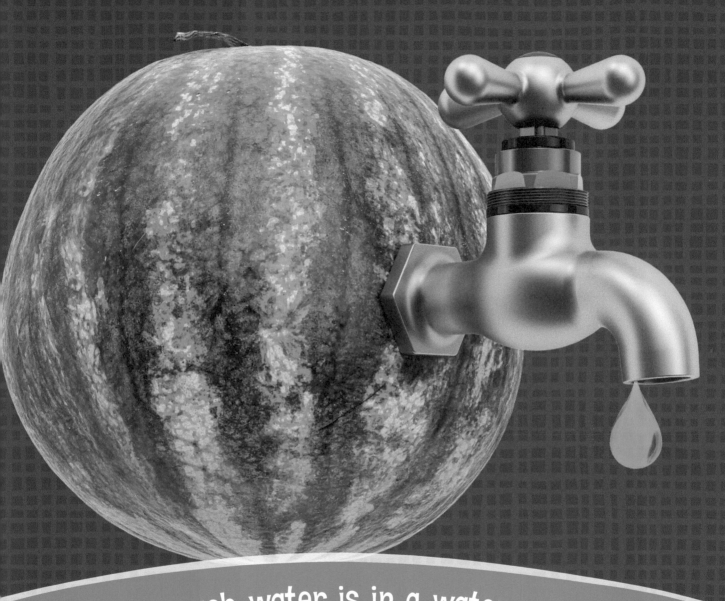

How much water is in a watermelon?

A watermelon lives up to its name, since each one is about 92 percent water. That's a lot of water! Watermelons also have lots of vitamins and minerals and a juicy, delicious taste.

Strawberries grow on runners, which are long stems that grow along the ground. At the end of each runner, a new plant forms. Hiding beneath the green leaves you'll find ripe, red strawberries.

How many oranges are in one glass of juice?

Some oranges are juicier than others. Depending on the size and type of oranges used, it takes about two to four oranges to make a small glass of juice.

How many different kinds of apples are there?

There are more than 7,000 varieties of apples!
They can be large or small, sweet or tart, and
different shades of red, yellow, or green.

And there are thousands of ways you can eat
them—in applesauce, apple pie, apple juice . . .
or right off the tree!

Why do potatoes have eyes?

"Eyes" is the name for the little sprouts that
sometimes appear on potatoes. These are actually
buds. If you bury the potato in the ground, new
potato plants will grow from the eyes.

How do bees help crops grow?

Bees gather pollen from plants to make food. As bees travel from plant to plant, they spread pollen. This is called pollination. It helps plants form the fruits we eat and the seeds we need to grow new crops.

Thanks, bees!

Fun Farm Facts!

Not all kinds of lettuce form heads. The leaves of loose leaf lettuce grow along a stalk. Loose leaf lettuce leaves may be green or red.

The United States is one of the top raisin-producing countries in the world. Almost all the raisins grown in the U.S. come from sunny California.

In the morning, sunflowers face east toward the rising sun. They follow the sun across the sky throughout the day. By evening, they are facing west toward the sunset.

The carrots we eat are actually the root of the carrot plant. Other root vegetables include beets, radishes, onions, and potatoes.

Watermelons come in many shapes, colors, and sizes. The outside may be dark green, light green, or gold. Inside they may be red, pink, orange, or even yellow!

Bees are important pollinators for many of the foods we eat. Some crops that depend on bees include almonds, apples, blueberries, melons, and cherries.

One orange tree produces an average of 100 to 300 or more oranges per year. Sweet!

Some of the more popular apple varieties include Red Delicious, Golden Delicious, Granny Smith, Gala, and Honeycrisp. Which kind do you like best?